A SINGLE LINE of footprints leads away from the golden sand beach of Ha'ena (red hot) Point on the North side of Kaua'i. Found in the luminous green of the hillside facing the beach is a succession of rock terraces where legend has it that Pele, Hawai'i's volcano goddess, danced for the high chief Lohiau. To the east, the valley of Wainiha (unfriendly water) was home to the, *Menehune*, a legendary race of small people, who worked only at night.

THE KALEIDOSCOPIC CLIFFS of Waimea Canyon, the "Grand Canyon of the Pacific," on Kaua'i's west side continue to amaze both scientists and spectators. Millions of years of erosion formed the earth-toned ridges. Three thousand six hundred feet deep, ten miles long, and one mile wide, the canyon began as a small crack on the side of the volcano. Now deserted, the canyon shows signs of early habitation. Man-made walls still stand and ancient petroglyphs are carved into the rocks. It is said that the canyon was home to the *Menehune*, a legendary race of physically short and clever people, who worked at night constructing ponds, roads and temples. If the work was not finished in one night, it was left unfinished forever. In the background Waipo'o Falls, a thick stream of foamy white, crashes down a cliff face, feeding into the headwaters of Waimea River.

BILLOWY WHITE CLOUDS hang over the dense green valley walls of the Nā Pali (the cliffs) Coast on Kaua'i's north side. Formed from a mammoth basalt volcanic dome, the rock formations are natural wonders, inspiring legends, secrets, and providing a home to rare Hawaiian plants. There is no road along Nā Pali Coast. It is accessible only by hiking trails or when the sea is calm, by boat. The majestic and untouched beauty of the Nā Pali Coast stands as a reminder of the Hawai'i of long ago.

LOOKING THROUGH THE trees and dense fern, the view from Kilohana at the end of the Alaka'i Swamp Trail in Koke'e is wondrous. Thick blankets of cloud seep into and rise out of the mountains, illuminating the green. Koke'e (to bend or to wind) State Park, located along Waimea Canyon Road on the west side of the island, was established in 1952. It is a 4,345 acre wilderness area where visitors can gaze at koa trees, mountain streams, and unique Hawaiian birds and flowers. The fragrant *mokihana* berry, the symbol for the island of Kaua'i, grows in the Koke'e uplands.

KAUA'I'S FIRST SUCCESSFUL sugar plantation was started in 1835 by three men from New England who obtained a fifty-year lease from King Kamehameha III for 980 acres of land in Kōloa near the southern tip of the island. Today, the only things left standing from the original mills are remnants of the boiling house and smokestack. The sugar plantation town of Kekaha (the place), north of Kōloa, is virtually free from tourism, a hot and dry bastion of steel and smoke. *Opposite page:* Irrigation furrows fill with water as a field is prepared for a new crop of sugar cane. *This page, top:* The rusted metal claws of a crane grab smoldering cane in a Kekaha field. *Middle:* Loaded down with cane, a "fuzzy" truck overflows from all sides. *Bottom:* The eerie yellow glow of Kekaha Sugar Mill at night.

FLANKED BY GREEN shrubs and the blue sea, Barking Sands beach is an oasis of white in the Waimea district on Kaua'i's west side. The beach runs fifteen miles between the sea cliffs at Polihale (house bosom) and Kekaha (the place), making it the longest continual beach in the islands. It is home to the U.S. Navy Pacific Missile Range Fleet Mobile Tracking Facility. During the dry seasons the sixty foot tall sand dunes at Barking Sands emit a loud "woofing" noise when they are slid down or walked upon.

TALL AND LANKY boat masts cast their reflection in the dark waters of Nāwiliwili (the *wiliwili* trees) Small Boat Harbor just south of Līhu'e (cold chill), Kaua'i's capital. In the 1850s Līhu'e started out as a village connected to Līhu'e Plantation and Grove Farm. The town grew and prospered into the busy government and commercial district it is today. In the background, the looming green cliffs of Hā'upu (recollection) Range stand a massive and watchful sentinel.

STREAMS OF WATER tumble over the craggy rock waterfall and into the mountain pool at Silver Falls Ranch. Located in the high interior valley of the Kalihi Wai ridge on Kaua'i's north shore, the ranch is a strictly equine facility, offering some of the most lush riding trails on the island. One can ride past winding streams and inhale the intoxicating scent of *'awapuhi melemele* (yellow ginger) wafting over the trails. In the background, the towering green cliffs of Kamo'okoa Ridge cut into the blue skies above.

Opposite page: DWARFED BY MOUNTAINS and flanked by trees, the white trimmed beams and burnished red-painted wood that make up the Anahola Baptist Church, are a throwback to earlier times. Located north of Līhuʻe on the eastern side of the island, the church was originally built by sugar plantation workers. Although Kauaʻi now bustles with business, these rural buildings are a lasting reminder of the Island's yesteryear.

KAUAʻI'S BUILDINGS, SOME of which have been renovated after Hurricane Iniki in 1992, reflect the island's diversity. *Top:* Waimea Foreign Church. *Middle:* Soto Store on the banks of Hanapēpē River. *Bottom:* The sun sets, casting rich yellows against a slow moving Hanapēpē afternoon.

MILLIONS OF WHITE salt crystals fill the Hanapēpē (crushed bay [due to landslides]) Salt Ponds, a brilliant contrast against the deep-red dirt fields. Water that is saltier than seawater is dipped from adjacent shallow wells and left to evaporate in the ponds until a dry crust forms. During the summer months, local families come to the ponds which have been passed down through the generations to collect the salt using nearly the same methods as the ancient Hawaiians. When gathered, the salt is often mixed with a special, finely powdered red clay (*alae*) which gives it a pinkish tinge. The salt is not sold commercially, but treasured by the friends and families of the saltmakers.

SUNSHINE BREAKS ACROSS the verdant mountainsides and terraced gardens of Limahuli (turned hand) Garden in Hā'ena near Kalalau (the straying) Valley on Kaua'i's northwest side. The dense green forest area of Limahuli Valley is home to many newly discovered species of rare, native Hawaiian plants. Kalalau, the longest valley on the Nā Pali coast, is the setting for one of the most intriguing Hawaiian legends. In 1889, Ko'olau, the most famous *paniolo* (cowboy) in Kaua'i's history, and his wife contracted leprosy. Instead of going to Moloka'i with all of the other leprosy victims, Ko'olau and his family fled to Kalalau Valley. Kaua'i's deputy sheriff set out to find Ko'olau himself, but was killed when Ko'olau shot him twice in the stomach. He and his family eluded capture and stayed in the valley until his death in 1896.

BRILLIANT PURPLE SPRIGS of *pukanawila* (bougainvillea) gaze down from the Hanapēpē Canyon Lookout onto the muted browns and greens of Hanapēpē Valley on Kauaʻi's south side. Opposite the lookout is the site of Kauaʻi's last major battle which took place in 1824. Kaumualiʻi, the Kauaʻi chief who exchanged hogs and yams with Vancouver in exchange for the name George (in honor of the King who ruled England in 1794), led an unsuccessful revolt against troops loyal to Kamehameha. Over one hundred rebels were reported to have died in the revolt.

PERCHED ON THE tip of a jagged rock formation at Māhāʻulepū (and falling together) on Kauaʻi's south shore, a stone meditates over the crashing waves. The south shore is known for its mild dry weather, gorgeous beaches and laid back lifestyle. Māhāʻulepū is one of the beaches comprising Kauaʻi's "Gold Coast."

Opposite page: WHITE AND BEAMING, the red-topped Kilauea Lighthouse, built in 1913, guided ships past Kaua'i and on to the Orient for over sixty years. The 52-foot-high lighthouse at Kaua'i's northern tip has the world's largest clamshell lens. When it was operating, the lighthouse sent out a double flash every ten seconds. The seemingly effortless orchestration of parts was an amazing feat—the moving parts weighed four tons! Replaced by an automatic beacon in 1976, the Kilauea Lighthouse closed and the surrounding area, now a National Wildlife Refuge, boasts the largest seabird colony in the main Hawaiian Islands.

THRIVING IN THEIR nesting site, *top:* a new born Laysan albatross chick surveys the world. *Middle:* The stately laysan albatross looks over its shoulder. *Bottom:* The red-footed booby squawks at the sky. The birds can be found at Kilauea Point National Wildlife Refuge.

THE SUN CREEPS up the emerald mountainsides overlooking Hanalei (crescent) Bay at sunrise. The largest bay on Kaua'i, Hanalei Bay, located on the island's north side, is the spot for summer yachting and winter surfing. Hanalei, a town which has managed to keep the modern world at bay and retain its old-time feel, holds a special place in Hawaiian hearts and is treasured by those living on Kaua'i. In 1873, English travel writer Isabella Bird described Hanalei's atmosphere as "so glorious that it was possible to think of nothing all day, but just allow oneself passively to drink in sensations of exquisite pleasure."

GRACEFUL AS SWANS, budding *kalo* (taro) plants rise out of the water, a stunning sight against the golden glow of a Hanalei sunset. Extending deep into Hanalei Valley, taro patches line the broad Hanalei River, flourishing in the moist terrain. Taro in Hanalei is still picked by hand, producing more than fifty percent of Hawai'i's crop. The lower 900 acres of the lush green valley is a National Wildlife Refuge administered by the U.S. Fish and Wildlife Service.

A SCENIC LANDSCAPE is mirrored in the calm waters of Hanalei River which flows through the center of Kaua'i's taro farms on its way to the ocean. At the end of the river where the water flows into the sea, surfers flock to the winter waves which can reach heights of up to twenty-five feet.